# THE CATHOLIC COMMUNITY IN ISLEWORTH

by

Stuart Bagnall

First published in Great Britain 2008 by:
Our Lady of Sorrows and St. Bridget of Sweden Catholic Church,
Memorial Square, 112 Twickenham Road, Isleworth TW7 6DL
W: www.stbridgets.org.uk


Second Edition 2015


This edition published by:
Our Lady of Sorrows and St. Bridget of Sweden Catholic Church,
an imprint of St. Mary's University, Twickenham

ISBN 978-0-950-14957-8


Cover Design by Colin Kyte 020 8892 7801
Artwork by Biggles Graphic Design 01243 583714


Printed by CreateSpace

2

# CONTENTS

*contents continued overleaf*

# CONTENTS *continued*

# INTRODUCTION –
# A ROMAN CATHOLIC STRONGHOLD?

In 1911, a Free Church minister turned down an invitation to offer himself as pastor of a local church because Isleworth was in his words:

"…a stronghold for Roman Catholics…"

and would not be fertile ground for his ministry. He may have been influenced by the recent opening of a large and distinctive Catholic church in a prominent position at the edge of the town centre. He may also have noticed the presence of a number of flourishing religious institutions including several convents. It is possible too that he was aware of the prominent involvement of several Catholic laymen in the management of local affairs. Fortunately, the Free Church concerned quickly found another candidate who was willing to serve in Isleworth.

I doubt that the local Catholics then, or ever, regarded Isleworth as a stronghold because they, like Catholics throughout Great Britain, saw themselves as a minority, which, if it were no longer actively persecuted was, at best, tolerated. Nevertheless it is true that Isleworth was home to a flourishing Catholic community.

This is a brief history of that community from small beginnings in the early 1700s to recent times but it begins with a crucial turning point, the centenary of which occurred in 2009.

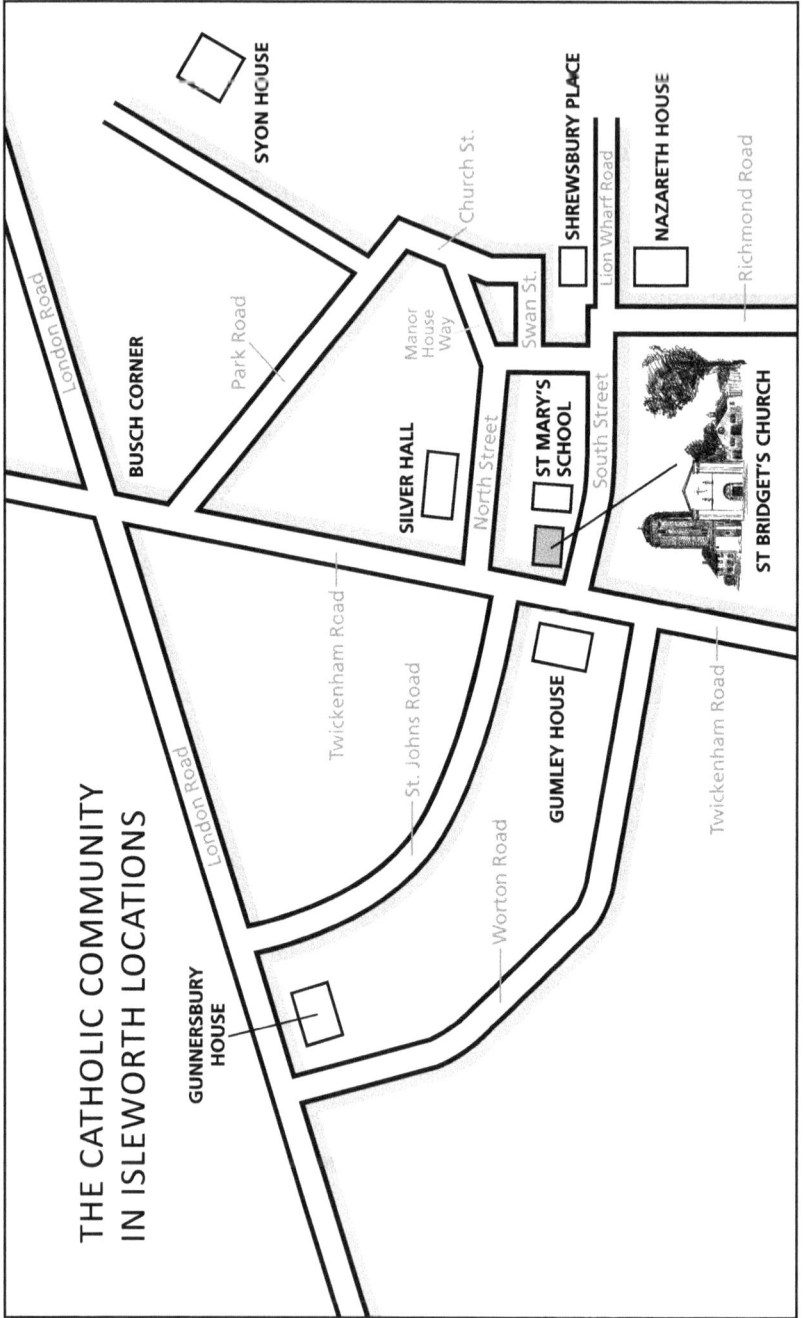

# THE CATHOLIC COMMUNITY
# IN ISLEWORTH LOCATIONS

SYON HOUSE

SHREWSBURY PLACE

NAZARETH HOUSE

Church St.

Lion Wharf Road

Richmond Road

BUSCH CORNER

London Road

Park Road

Manor House Way

Swan St.

SILVER HALL

North Street

ST MARY'S SCHOOL

South Street

ST BRIDGET'S CHURCH

Twickenham Road

St. Johns Road

GUMLEY HOUSE

Twickenham Road

London Road

Worton Road

GUNNERSBURY HOUSE

6

# FATHER GREEN'S LEGACY

The parish of Our Lady of Sorrows and St. Bridget, as we think of it today, emerged in the period 1906 to 1929 under the leadership of Father Eric Green (1870-1929). However, Father Green, a modest and well-loved priest, would have been first to acknowledge that he was building on firm foundations laid down over the previous 200 years. He came to Isleworth in 1906 from the Westminster Cathedral parish and found a large and growing Catholic population (he estimated it at 1,200-1,300[1]) served by a small back street chapel with a capacity of 200. The congregation was socially very diverse. It included a number of influential, talented and wealthy lay people but, like the other Catholic communities in England at the time, most of its members were poor.

*Father Eric Francis Green (1870-1929)*

In addition to the public chapel, there were several convents (including Gumley House, Nazareth House, Gunnersbury House and Silver Hall), a school for boys attached to the chapel and one for girls attached to Gumley House and managed by the nuns. There was also a convent boarding school for girls established within Gumley House itself.

Father Green was a young, able and enterprising priest who had a gift for mobilising support. The confidence of the Catholic community was growing at this time and he was prepared to take initiatives that would raise its public profile. Like the Church in general, he gave priority to education and

---

[1] The total population of the district at this time was about 25,000.

set about the provision of a new building for the boys' school. He simultaneously organized the construction of the new church. Catholic chapels built before full emancipation in 1829 had been discreetly located in back streets. The old Isleworth chapel at Shrewsbury Place was out of sight behind a high wall. The new church was large and visible. It was completed and opened in 1909. As the church was debt-free, consecration followed quickly in 1910. The construction of this church is symbolic of the emergence, literally, from behind high walls of a community growing in assurance.

# ORIGINS OF THE COMMUNITY

*St. Bridget's Church, Rectory and Hall in 1962 with the War Memorial in front and the roof of the 1907 school building visible behind* (Photo: Martin Russell)

The Isleworth Mission to which Father Green had been appointed went back to the reign of King George II, making Isleworth one of the oldest post-Reformation Catholic communities in England. Surviving registers of baptisms prove it was in existence in 1746; some sources say it began as early as 1675.[2] There were certainly individual Catholics in West Middlesex in the 1600s but they did not in any sense constitute a community. The Elizabethan Settlement of religion had effectively eliminated Roman Catholicism in this area. A survey of papists [as Catholics were called] conducted for the Anglican Bishop of London in 1706 reported only three living in Isleworth, including a dancing master called Mr. Callys.[3]

Isleworth at this time was a small riverside town dominated by Syon House, one of the estates of the Duke of Northumberland. Around the edge of the town, there were several lesser mansions. One of these was known as Shrewsbury House or Shrewsbury Place. It was on the Richmond Road in what is now Lion Wharf Road and was owned by the Earls of Shrewsbury whose family name was Talbot.[4] The Talbots were one of

[2] Catholic Record Society *Miscellanea XIII* LONDON.
[3] Guildhall Library Manuscript 9800.
[4] The Earls professed the faith openly from 1718 - see Robbins M. *Middlesex* CHICHESTER 2003.

the families that had for the most part remained Catholic throughout the penal period. The Catholic community in Isleworth had its origin in the domestic setting of the Shrewsbury Place household. The Talbots maintained a chaplain there who ministered to the family and their servants and, as the surviving registers show, to local Catholics not only in the town but also throughout West Middlesex and the nearby parts of Surrey. A small permanent chapel dedicated to St. Mary and St. Bridget of Sweden was provided within the house.

The first chaplain of whom there is a record is the Revd. John Matthews alias Williams. Priests at this time found it useful to have an alias in an attempt to confuse the authorities. The legal situation of Catholics in England up until the late 1700s was that they could hold their religion in private but could not practise it publicly. Under the penal laws, places of worship, schools and religious houses were all illegal. Priests were prohibited from exercising their ministry and could be imprisoned or exiled if convicted.

*Shrewsbury Place, Isleworth*

John Matthews came from an old English Catholic family in Hampshire. He had trained for the priesthood at Douai College in France[5] and by 1702 was working in London where two

---

[5] All Catholic priests trained abroad at this time.

years later he was arrested and gaoled in Newgate prison for saying Mass. After his release Matthews became chaplain to Lady Shrewsbury at Isleworth and lived there until his death in 1744, when he was succeeded by another Douai-trained priest, the Revd. Richard Kendal. John Matthews was buried in All Saints' churchyard on the 11th September 1744.[6]

## FROM CHAPLAINCY TO MISSION

Until the formal restoration of the Roman Catholic hierarchy in 1850, England was treated as mission territory administered by bishops who reported directly to Rome. In 1741, the then Catholic missionary bishop for the London District, Richard Challoner, called at Shrewsbury Place on his way to conduct a visitation of Berkshire. He returned in 1743 and again in 1747 to administer the sacrament of Confirmation.[7]

The Talbot family itself produced two missionary bishops for the Catholic Church in England. James Talbot was born at Shrewsbury Place in Isleworth in 1726. He and his younger brother Thomas [born 1727] became priests and eventually were appointed bishops, James for the London area [in succession to Challoner] and Thomas for the Midlands. In 1771 James had the dubious honour of being the last Roman Catholic priest to be indicted in England for performing his priestly duties. The court was sympathetic to the accused and the judge threw out the case, citing a supposed lack of evidence.

Eventually, the Talbots left Isleworth but they retained ownership of the property and let it to an Irish gentleman called Thaddeus O'Flaherty. Richard Kendal continued his ministry

---

[6] Catholics were normally buried in parish churchyards at this time.
[7] CRS *Miscellanea XIII*.

with Mr. O'Flaherty's support. By 1758, the house was also being used as a school - Isleworth has long been a centre of Catholic education. The schoolmistress was a Mrs. Chitty and Richard Kendal was himself a teacher of some distinction. By 1770, the house had become a "school for boys of the Roman Catholic persuasion" [about 60 in number].[9]

Caution was necessary as long as the penal laws remained in place but they were not always rigorously enforced and limited activity did continue even under these conditions. In 1758, the Isleworth Vestry, which at that time was the local authority for both religious and civil matters, voted to ask the magistrates to close the chapel and school at Shrewsbury Place because they seemed to pose a threat to the Church of England. Mr. O'Flaherty objected that the Catholics were peaceful citizens who did not deserve this treatment. The Brentford magistrates agreed with O'Flaherty and the case was quietly dropped. Even so Richard Kendal moved away and was replaced by the Revd. John Exley. Exley served at Isleworth until shortly before his death in 1778.

In 1767, the Church of England nationally was being attacked in the Press for failing to counter an alleged alarming growth in the number of Roman Catholics in the country. To ascertain the facts, the Anglican bishops made a census of Catholics in their dioceses.[10] It was successful in refuting the accusations because, overall, the survey showed that the growth in the number of Catholics had been very modest and posed no threat. The census is especially interesting because it was very thorough and gives us a glimpse of the Isleworth Catholics at the time. The vicar reported one priest, 31 female and 28

[9] Brewer J. N. *London and Middlesex* LONDON 1816.
[10] Worrall E. S. ed. *Returns of Papists 1767* LONDON 1989.

male Catholics. They included nine gentlewomen, ten domestic servants, several tradesmen [two shoemakers, a cook, a carpenter, a glazier, a grocer, a tailor and a gardener] and labourers, as well as their wives and children. This was the second largest concentration in West Middlesex after Hammersmith and although it represents a substantial growth from the three reported in 1706, Catholics remained a tiny minority of the whole population. The survey found only about 400 Catholics in the whole of West Middlesex.

The missioner from 1778 to 1790 was the Revd. Robert Tommins. He was succeeded by Father William Allen of the Society of Jesus who served until 1810. One member of the congregation at this time was the wife of the distinguished English actor David Garrick [1717-1779]. Garrick came from French Protestant stock but in 1749 he married a celebrated Austrian dancer named Eva Marie Veigel, who was a Catholic. In 1754, Garrick built a villa beside the Thames at Hampton as their summer home and, when in residence there, Mrs. Garrick travelled regularly to services at Isleworth until her death in 1822.[11]

Mr. O'Flaherty died in July 1790 aged 93 and was buried in All Saints' churchyard.[12]

About 1797, Lord Shrewsbury commissioned a surveyor named George Cloake of Turnham Green to construct a chapel and associated apartments on part of the Shrewsbury Place site.[13] Lord Shrewsbury then asked Cloake to supervise the demolition of Shrewsbury Place itself. Cloake subsequently purchased the site with the exception of the plot of land on which the

[11] Robbins M *Middlesex* CHICHESTER 2003.
[12] Aungier G. *The History and Antiquities of Syon Monastery, Isleworth and Hounslow* LONDON 1840.
[13] This important discovery was made by local historian Kevin Brown in the course of examining records kept by the Sisters of Nazareth at their headquarters in Hammersmith.

new chapel stood. Lord Shrewsbury retained ownership of the chapel until 1824 when he formally handed it over to the church authorities.[14]

This means that Isleworth had one of the first free-standing Catholic chapels in post-Reformation England.

The atmosphere in the country at this period was generally tolerant and the government was gradually, step by cautious step, lifting the penalties that had been imposed on Catholics. In 1791, new legislation had permitted Catholics to open public chapels, subject to registration.[15] The Isleworth chapel was duly registered.

In 1810, a new missioner was appointed. He was the Revd. Anthony Wareing [1780-1854] who had trained at the English College in Lisbon. He was to serve in Isleworth for 44 years. Anthony Wareing was a Lancashire man and something of a personality. He was a keen and skilful angler. He was eventually barred from local fishing competitions to give others the chance of winning.

The published Shrewsbury Place registers, covering baptisms for the period 1745 to 1835, show that the chapel served a wide area including Richmond, Brentford, Twickenham, Teddington, Kingston, Whitton, Hounslow and Southall. The social mix was much as had been reported in the census of 1767, with tradesmen and servants and their families forming the majority but with a few members of the nobility and the gentry appearing too. The community was growing; its numbers increased by conversions and the arrival of Irish workers and their families, especially in the aftermath of the Great Famine

[14] Reynolds S. A *History of the County of Middlesex [Victoria County History]* Vol. III LONDON 1962.
[15] The Catholic Relief Act 1791.

caused by the failure of the potato crop in 1846 and 1847. When the French royal family was forced into exile and the Orleans princes settled in Twickenham, they too came under the care of the Isleworth mission. The mission served exiles and migrants from abroad whether royal or destitute without losing its essentially English character.

There is a sense of continuity in the registers as the same family names occur repeatedly, spanning the generations, notably the Strongitharms of Twickenham, the Taskers of Richmond and the Clarks of Isleworth. Over the years, the proportion of Irish names increases as migrants came and found work locally.

## THE NUNS ARRIVE

In 1841 a major development occurred in the Catholic life of Isleworth, the beneficial consequences of which are still felt strongly today. The modern schools, St. Mary's Junior, Infants & Nursery and Gumley House trace their origin to the establishment of the Gumley House convent by the Society of the Faithful Companions of Jesus in that year. The Society had been founded in France in 1820 by Mme. d'Houet, to provide education for children of all social classes, the fees of the better-off parents subsidising the schools provided for the poor. Mme d'Houet had already taken over an existing school founded by French exiles in London at Somers Town and had opened schools for poor children at Hampstead and Tottenham. She now wanted to open a boarding school in the country to attract the daughters of the 'well to do' as potential recruits to the Society who would serve as teachers. The Faithful Companions of Jesus were among the first of the new active religious orders of women to begin work in England and their Isleworth convent was one of the first to be opened since the Reformation.

Mme. d'Houet's personal chaplain, the Abbé Nerinckx, and Anthony Wareing were good friends and they worked together to purchase for the Society the Georgian mansion known as Gumley House from a Quaker lady called Mrs. Angell, who was the widow of the lessee of the Isleworth Flour Mill. Wareing became the first chaplain to the convent.

*An aerial view of Gumley House about 1890*

A touching advertisement for the boarding school appeared for many years in the annual Laity's Directory under the section allocated to Ladies Schools in Communities. It is worth reproducing in full from the 1850 Directory.

The advertisement emphasises the essentially French character of the school at that time and incidentally reveals that the nuns teaching there were drawn from several European countries.

The boarding school was successful in attracting the daughters of the 'well to do' and by 1855, there were more than 100 young ladies in residence. The granddaughters of the Duc d'Orleans[16] were among the pupils at this time.

---

[16] Louis Philippe, Duc d'Orleans. French nobleman living in exile with his family in Twickenham. See Cashmore T. *The Orleans Family in Twickenham* TWICKENHAM 1989.

## Gumley House, Isleworth

*The Religious Ladies, established for the last nine years at Gumley House, Isleworth, continue to offer to the public the many advantages to be procured by a continental education, combined with residence in England.*

*Gumley House is very agreeably situated; the gardens and pleasure grounds are truly beautiful, spacious and walled-in. The distance from London is likewise very convenient to parents and friends being about eight miles from Hyde Park Corner.*

*The French, English, Italian, and German languages are taught by natives. The French language is chiefly spoken, and as the ladies of the house are principally of that nation, it may not improperly be called a French establishment.*

*Terms for English, French, Italian, German, geography, the use of the globes, botany, history, writing, arithmetic, useful and ornamental needlework, £25 per annum. Music, drawing and dancing are extras. The pension to be paid quarterly in advance. A quarter's notice to be given previous to the removal of a pupil. A vacation is allowed at Midsummer, but no extra charge for young ladies who remain in the establishment during that period.*

*For further particulars apply to Madame D'Houet, or Madame De la Rochefoucald, Gumley House, Isleworth; the Revd. A. Wareing, Isleworth; Madame J. Guillemet; or the Revd. John Nerinckx, Clarendon Square, Somers-town.*

Mme. d'Houet's boarding schools were also effective in encouraging vocations and subsidising the schools for the poor. The nuns served people of all social classes ranging from foreign royalty to some of the poorest families in the country.

Mme. d'Houet is reported as being very taken with Gumley House and Isleworth. She left her sisters there a statue known as 'Our Lady of the Class' from which she took great personal inspiration. It can be seen in the convent to this day.

# THE MISSION EXPANDS

In March 1851, a national Census of Religion was conducted as part of the usual ten-yearly Census of Population.[17] It was officially intended to discover whether the means of "spiritual instruction" had kept pace with the growth in the population. Anthony Wareing reported that the Isleworth Catholic chapel had seats for 50 and standing room for 50. The estimated number attending service on the 30th March in that year was 70-80 and the average for the previous six months was 80.

Anthony Wareing died in 1854 and was buried in the Gumley House convent cemetery.

When Rome restored the Catholic hierarchy in England and Wales in September 1850, Isleworth became part of the new Archdiocese of Westminster. The restoration of the hierarchy did not immediately lead to the establishment of territorial parishes - this was not begun till 1918. As an interim arrangement, some missions were designated as rectories in which the priest had some security of tenure.[18] Isleworth was one of these. The first missionary rector was Francis Weld [1819-1898]. Weld was a member of an aristocratic family that, like the Talbots, had remained Catholic after the Reformation. Before he came to Isleworth, he had served as secretary to his uncle, Cardinal Thomas Weld, in the Roman Curia and had been granted the honorary title of Monsignor. On his uncle's death he had the opportunity to pursue a career in the Vatican but chose instead to do pastoral work in England. Before coming to Isleworth, he worked for ten years in Cornwall.

[17] The National Archives.
[18] Norman E. R. *The English Catholic Church in the Nineteenth Century* OXFORD 1984.

On arrival in Isleworth in 1854, Mgr. Weld decided that the tiny chapel at Shrewsbury Place, which measured 16 feet by 40 feet, was no longer adequate and he replaced it at his own expense with a larger chapel on the same site. The earlier building was retained as a sacristy.[19] Mgr. Weld modified the dedication to The Immaculate Conception and St. Bridget. He also opened a school for boys and the following year he provided a building for it at his own expense next to the chapel.[20] The first master was William Barnwell.[21] There was already a day school for local girls provided by the Faithful Companions of Jesus in their convent. After 1844 it had its own dedicated building. By 1881-2, both schools were receiving grants from the local authority. They had a combined roll of 113 pupils. In 1889, the Gumley nuns opened a mixed infants department.

*The sanctuary of the 1854 chapel*

The new chapel consisted of a nave and galleries with accommodation for about 200. Lulworth Castle, the ancestral mansion of the Weld family, has a Georgian Neo-classical chapel, the first free standing Catholic chapel to be built in England after the Reformation. It seems likely from the

[19] Kelly B. W. *Historical Notes on English Catholic Missions* LONDON 1907.
[20] Reynolds S. A *History of the County of Middlesex [Victoria County History]* Vol. III LONDON 1962.
[21] Post Office Directory 1855.

description and a surviving photograph that the new Isleworth chapel was designed in a simpler version of this style.

Mgr. Weld served the community for 44 years and amidst giving retreats and preaching missions found time to write a popular devotional work called *Divine Love, and the Love of God's Most Blessed Mother*, which was first published in 1873.

He was not the only writer active in the mission. A visitor to the parish in the period 1868-1870 was the poet Gerard Manley Hopkins, who was then a novice at Manresa House, the Jesuit house of studies at Roehampton. Brother Gerard regularly came to Isleworth and other Middlesex missions on Sunday afternoons to teach the local children their catechism.[22]

One of the property developments that helped to boost the population of Isleworth was the Spring Grove Estate, developed by the businessman Henry Daniel Davis on land to the north of the London Road. One of the families that came to live there was the Willmotts. Frederick Willmott, a solicitor, married Ellen Fell, the daughter of a lace merchant, at Holy Trinity, Brook Green, Hammersmith in 1856. Ellen came from a Catholic family; Frederick was probably a convert. They were a very wealthy couple and took one of the new mansions in The Grove as their home. They lived in Isleworth for 20 years and worshipped at St. Bridget's. Their three daughters Ellen, Rose and Ada Mary were all baptised by Mgr. Weld and the girls later attended the school at Gumley House. Ada died in 1876 at the age of 8 of diphtheria and was buried in the convent burial ground. Shortly after this tragic event, the family moved to Warley Place in Essex but kept in touch with Mgr. Weld, who had become a family friend. Ellen Willmott [1858-1934] went

---

[22] Martin R. B. *Gerard Manley Hopkins: A Very Private Life* LONDON 1992.

on to become an award-winning gardener. In 1897 she was awarded the Royal Horticultural Society's Victoria Medal and in 1904 she was among the first women to be elected to the Linnean Society.[23]

Another active and influential member of the congregation was James Britten [1846-1924]. He was a convert from the Church of England who worshipped at St. Bridget's where he was the choirmaster for many years. He was a botanist by profession and was a curator at the Natural History Museum from 1871-1909. Like Ellen Willmott, Britten was a Fellow of the Linnean Society. From 1884 to 1922 he was the Honorary Secretary of the Catholic Truth Society. The CTS had originally been set up by the energetic Father Herbert [later Cardinal] Vaughan in 1868 with the twin aims of instructing Catholics in their faith and dispelling some the prejudice and misinformation that surrounded them. With Vaughan's elevation to the hierarchy in 1872, the Society had become dormant. Britten re-established it in 1884 with Vaughan's blessing. Britten also involved himself in social work locally and in London and his letters on church matters were frequently published in the London Times. In 1897, Rome acknowledged his work by the award of a Papal knighthood.

## NEW MISSIONS IN MIDDLESEX

After 1850, the population of West Middlesex continued to grow and with it the Catholic community expanded. New missions were opened in the area formerly served from Isleworth - Chiswick [1853], Brentford [1856], Sunbury [1862], Teddington

---

[23] Main source: Article by Mary Brown, March 1997 issue of the *Honeslaw Chronicle*, the journal of the Hounslow & District History Society.

[1882] and Twickenham [1883]. Richmond in Surrey had its own mission from 1793.[24]

Mgr. Weld himself was instrumental in founding the Hounslow chapel. He presided over a meeting held in a public house in Hounslow in early June 1883 to consider ways and means for building a church there. There was already the nucleus of a community because local civilians had been hearing Mass with the soldiers in the Barracks for some years. The meeting decided that a public chapel should be provided for the town and a collection at the meeting produced more than £20 towards the cost. A site was found in the Bath Road and building went ahead. The new chapel, dedicated to the soldiers' saints: St. Michael and St. Martin, was opened by Cardinal Manning on the 24th August 1886.[25]

Mgr. Weld died in 1898 after a long period of ill health. He was buried at Downside Abbey in Somerset. He had had a long association with the Abbey and had paid for some of the buildings there. From 1882 he had been assisted by one or more curates and it was one of these, the Revd. Thomas Gorman [1840-1907] who succeeded him as rector.

Isleworth continued to grow and there was work in the market gardens and in local industries. It combined the opportunity for employment with ready access to a place of Catholic worship and so it attracted Catholic migrants from Ireland and to a lesser extent Italy. The newcomers ranged from the destitute and illiterate to the well educated and enterprising.

The Weathers family was among the latter. Philip Weathers and his wife Mary came from County Cork. He was born in about

[24] See Hughes N. *The Richmond Catholic Mission 1791-1826* RICHMOND 1991.
[25] Kelly B. W. *Historical Notes on English Catholic Missions* LONDON 1907.

1831. His wife was 10 years younger. They settled in Isleworth in 1875 and had six children, four boys and two girls. People from Cork are said to be the most industrious and businesslike in Ireland and this family certainly bears that out. One of the sons, John, trained in horticulture at Kew Gardens and in 1893 became the Assistant Secretary of the Royal Horticultural Society.[26] In 1899, he opened a nursery in the Twickenham Road opposite its junction with St. John's Road, which continued in business until the early 1920s. He was the founder and editor of the Isleworth Citizen, an entertaining local monthly journal. His brothers, Brian and Joseph ran the newsagent's and confectioner's shop at 15, St. John's Road for many years. They were all active in local politics and stout defenders of the interests of Isleworth against the growing influence of its neighbour, Hounslow. John was an Urban District Councillor; Joseph was a Middlesex County Councillor. Members of the family still worship at St. Bridget's.

Another prominent parishioner with Irish connections was Patrick Murphy. He had been born in America in 1854 and had been taken to Ireland as a boy. He settled in Isleworth in about 1889 and became the manager of the Isleworth Flour Mill. His home was in Woodlands Grove. He was a larger-than-life character who sported a substantial handlebar moustache and a white Stetson hat. He was a bachelor who devoted himself to public service. He was a Justice of the Peace and chairman of the Poor Law Guardians [1928-1933]. He was sometime chairman of the Borough Education Committee and a manager of St. Mary's College [Gumley House] and the St. Mary's Schools. He was also a County Councillor.[27] He was a great

---

[26] Main source: Article by Mary Brown, Sept 1993 issue of the *Honeslaw Chronicle*, the journal of the Hounslow & District History Society.

[27] Hounslow Local Studies Collection *Isleworth Citizen* April 1925 and August 1931.

committeeman and in one of his election addresses he claimed that he had attended 560 meetings in the previous three years. He was a member of the Isleworth Philanthropic Society and a trustee of the Isleworth Charities.[28] He died in 1934 and is buried in Isleworth Cemetery. In his will he left a bequest for the foundation of a boys Catholic grammar school in Isleworth which eventually was used to establish Gunnersbury Grammar School in Brentford.

Many of the new arrivals prospered but not all. Magdala Road behind South Street became an enclave of the Irish poor and the 1881 Census reveals occupation of the cottages there at levels that scarcely seem credible to us. For example, one small house contained a young married couple and their four children plus an elderly relative and four lodgers. The Magdala Road area gained a certain notoriety and one of the local magistrates had a reputation of being unsympathetic to the Irish. When the Metropolitan Police moved their Isleworth station from Church Street in 1873, it was to a site in Worple Road just opposite its junction with Magdala Road but that may be pure coincidence.

## DEVELOPMENTS IN THE SCHOOLS

The 1902 Education Act put voluntary [i.e. church] schools on the rates, but subject to inspection. This was clearly a welcome development for Catholics but it led in 1904 to the existing boys' school building being condemned by the inspectors as unsuitable. Work on the new building to replace it began as we have seen in 1907.

---

[28] *The Universe* 22 June 1934.

In 1923 the St. Mary's Infant's Department became mixed but the boys' and girls' schools were not finally amalgamated until 1948. From then both sets of buildings were used - those attached to the convent as the Junior Mixed and Infants, those in South Street as the Seniors - and it remained an 'all age' school until Archbishop Myers Secondary Modern School [now St. Mark's School] was opened in Hounslow in 1960. In 1962, the Junior Mixed and Infants School moved on to the former Senior School site with the original building incorporated into what was substantially a new school. In 1970 the new school hall was built and in 1981 the Nursery Unit was added.

Gumley House had begun taking day pupils in 1890 in what was then known as St. Mary's College. In 1920, the day school was reorganized as a voluntary secondary school and, in 1922, it was provided with a new building known as 'School Block'. It became comprehensive in 1966 and further expansion followed.[29]

# MORE CONVENTS

By 1890 Gumley House was a well-established and respected part of local Catholic life. It was soon to be joined by a number of other religious institutions.

### Nazareth House

The Catholic bishops in Victorian England were acutely aware of the deficiencies in the social care offered by the Church. Cardinal Wiseman invited a recently founded French congregation of nuns to send sisters to the London district to

---

[29] Gumley House Convent School Prospectus.

provide care for orphans and the elderly. Five sisters came from Paris and, eventually, settled at Hammersmith in what is now the Nazareth House there. Soon afterwards the Hammersmith community detached itself from the mother house and became in effect a new independent congregation, the Poor Sisters of Nazareth.[30] *Poor* because they depended on alms solicited by "begging nuns" from Catholics and non-Catholics alike; *Nazareth* because their twin objectives were personal sanctification and care of the poor on the pattern of the Holy Family of Nazareth.[31]

By 1890 the Order was expanding and was looking for a suitable house with grounds not too far from Hammersmith. Isleworth House, a mansion set in extensive grounds next to the River Thames on the edge of the town, was offered for sale in 1892. It was bought by Miss Clarke and Miss Jones, who were Sisters of the Order, and by October of that year, three sisters and six children had transferred from Hammersmith and founded the convent. The retired Auxiliary Bishop of Westminster, William Weathers,[32] joined the community as resident chaplain in 1893. He died in 1895. An industrial school for girls in a tall red brick building was added in 1899. The Industrial Schools Act of 1866 provided for the establishment of training schools for children in care to give them a trade by which they might support themselves. In the case of girls, the training seems to have been mainly for domestic service. An official report of 1913 described the Nazareth House industrial school as "an admirable institution in every respect".

In 1901, work began on a new chapel to the design of A. S. Pugin-Powell, a relative of the more famous A. W. N. Pugin.

---

[30] Evinson D. *Pope's Corner* LONDON 1980.
[31] Anson P. *Religious Orders and Congregations of Great Britain and Ireland* WORCESTER 1949.
[32] The bishop was not, as far as I can tell, related to the Isleworth Weathers family.

The chapel, dedicated to St. Augustine, was located on the first floor of a building that also provided accommodation for male residents on the ground floor. The altar was donated by Mrs. Catherine Feres Macdonnell, a resident of the home, who also paid for a new wing of the house to provide accommodation for 120 "friendless girls, out of situations". Mrs. Macdonnell died in 1913 and was buried in the convent cemetery. The Industrial School closed in 1922 and the building was adapted for use as a home for children in need. This continued until 1985 when it was again adapted, this time as a residential home for older people. In 2002, due to the decline in vocations to the religious life and the requirement to meet new standards of accommodation, the convent and home were closed. A plan to develop the property as a 'care village' for the elderly under the general supervision of the Order fell through and the site has been sold.

## Gunnersbury House, London Road[33]

Gunnersbury House was a Victorian mansion located at the junction of Bridge Road with London Road. In 1896 it was owned by a Mrs. Anne Monteith, a widow who was a convert to Catholicism and wanted the house to be used for religious purposes. She offered it to the Little Company of Mary, a recent English foundation of sisters dedicated to the spiritual and nursing care of the dying. The founder and superior of the order Mother Mary Potter was keen to accept the gift because she wanted to move her novitiate from the cramped first house of the order at Hyson Green in Nottingham to somewhere more suitable. After negotiations that took account of the donor's insistence that she and her daughter should live in the house

[33] Healy E. *The Life of Mother Mary Potter* LONDON 1935, Dougherty P. *Mother Mary Potter, Foundress of the Little Company of Mary* LONDON 1961 and Campion M. *A Place of Springs* PRIVATELY PRINTED 1977.

and that a ward for "crippled children" should be provided as part of the scheme, the first nuns took up residence in 1897. In the event, the donor and her daughter did not remain long in the house. Mother Mary considered Gunnersbury House to be too remote from the public chapel in Old Isleworth, so the nuns installed a prefabricated corrugated iron chapel next to the house and the Archbishop of Westminster gave permission for the Blessed Sacrament to be reserved there. From 1899, the novitiate was based here. At the time of the 1901 Census there were 17 sisters based at the convent, engaged in nursing the sick in their own homes and caring for children and the elderly within the house.

After 1901, the convent had a distinguished resident chaplain in Dr. Edward Bagshawe, the retired bishop of Nottingham. Dr. Bagshawe had been instrumental in supporting Mother Mary Potter's efforts to establish her order and although they had come into conflict more than once over the years, they were finally reconciled after his retirement and he spent his last years at Gunnersbury House as chaplain to the sisters. He died there in 1915. As time went on, Gunnersbury House became insufficient for the Order's needs and in 1922 they acquired the more substantial Hillingdon Court near Uxbridge and moved the community including the novitiate from Isleworth. Gunnersbury House was sold and used as industrial premises for the next fifty years, being finally demolished and redeveloped as an office block and housing in the 1970s. A few of the large trees fronting the London Road are all that remains of the garden but the work done by these dedicated women was remembered long after they had moved away from Isleworth.

## Carmelite Convent, North Street[34]

A community of Carmelite nuns resided in Lillie Road, Hammersmith from 1867 in a purpose built convent. By the end of the century, the location was no longer suitable so they sold the site and in 1899 they purchased Silver Hall in North Street, Isleworth, which had been the home of the Misses Saunders.[35] The Carmelite nuns are contemplative and are enclosed to allow them to concentrate on their vocation of prayer. The purchase had been arranged by a third party because the nuns believed, incorrectly as it turned out, that the rules of enclosure prohibited them from viewing the prospective property in person. After moving, they quickly realised to their dismay that the property was quite unsuitable for their purposes. Nevertheless they set about making the best of the situation and received much help from the sisters at Gumley House. Being enclosed they had little contact with the wider community.

Their search for a suitable site in the London area took five years but eventually they found one in Bridge Lane, Hendon and they had a new convent built there.

The Carmelites left Isleworth in 1908 for the new convent in Hendon, where they remained until recently.[36] Silver Hall itself was demolished in 1950 but for many years after that the painted words 'Carmelite Convent' could be discerned on the pillars of the street gate. The site has now been laid out as a public park.

---

[34] I am indebted to the Carmelite Community of the Holy Family for the information in this section.
[35] Evinson D. *Pope's Corner* LONDON 1980 p. 61.
[36] They are now based in Preston, Lancashire.

# Religious Houses in Osterley

Three religious houses in Osterley were originally within the boundaries of the Isleworth mission. Two of them belonged to French missionary societies that had been expelled from France in 1905 by the anti-clerical government: the Congregation of the Missions [known as the Vincentians] and the Missions Etrangeres de Paris. They each purchased large Victorian mansions the Spring Grove area. The Vincentian community of four or five priests opened its small chapel dedicated to St. Vincent in Witham Road to the local population. This eventually developed into the present Osterley parish.[37]

In 1911, the English Province of the Society of Jesus [the Jesuits], a religious body of priests and brothers dedicated to teaching and missionary work, acquired Thornbury House in Thornbury Road as a retreat house for lay people. The acquisition had been made possible by a large donation from Mme. Léonie Blumenthal. The house was renamed Campion House in 1915. After the First World War it was used as a training college for mature men with what are known as 'late vocations' to the priesthood. The first such students were men whose education had been interrupted by the First World War. Campion House prepared hundreds of men for further studies on their way to the priesthood and it commanded respect throughout the church in the British Isles. In later years, while continuing to prepare candidates for the priesthood, the college began to train lay people for ministry and at the same time it resumed its original function as a retreat centre. The late Cardinal Hume once described it as "one of the truly great institutions of the Church in this country". Sadly, with the

---

[37] For the history of Osterley Catholic parish see: Weiler T. *A Parish History 1936-1996 St Vincent de Paul, Osterley* OSTERLEY 1996.

decline in vocations to the priesthood and the reorganization of seminary training there was no longer the need for a college with such extensive residential accommodation. Despite the popularity and success of both the retreat programme and the training of lay people for pastoral work, the Jesuits decided to close Campion House and sell the site. It closed in 2004 and the site has been redeveloped. The history of the college has been comprehensively chronicled by Mrs. Ann Smith in her book *The Story of Campion House, Osterley*, published in 2004.

## FROM MISSION TO PARISH

Father Gorman's tenure was destined to be short by Isleworth standards. He suffered from ill health and had to retire in 1906. Nevertheless he planned for the expansion of the mission and began preparations for the initiatives that Father Green was soon to put into effect.

A survey of the religious life of London in 1902/03 revealed that the congregation of the Isleworth Catholic chapel on the survey day was 339; 84 men, 123 women and 132 children.[38] Another source[39] estimated that the total Catholic population of the district at about 500. In the district of Heston and Isleworth, the Catholics were the largest non-Anglican group with about 14% of the church attendance. Churchgoing was already a minority activity with less than 30% of the district's total population attending any service.

On arrival in 1906, Father Green lost no time in promoting three major initiatives, a new school, a new church and an annual outdoor procession.

[38] Mudie Smith E. R. *The Religious Life of London* LONDON 1904.
[39] Kelly B. W. *Historical Notes on English Catholic Missions* LONDON 1907.

# The New School

*The 1908 boys' school building as it is today*

The boy's school building at Shrewsbury Place had been condemned as inadequate by the local authority in 1904. Fortunately, the Misses Saunders, formerly of Silver Hall in North Street, had donated a site opposite Gumley House at the junction of South Street and Twickenham Road to the Catholic community. It was large enough for a new school and a new church. The frontage of the site was allocated to the church. Work on the church and the new school building began in 1907 and the boys moved into the school in 1908.[40] The school building survives and forms part the present St. Mary's.

## The New Church

Construction of the church, which was largely financed by Mrs. Catherine Feres Macdonnell, then residing at Nazareth House, took longer but it was ready for occupation in April 1909. The last service in the old chapel was held on Sunday May 2nd 1909. On Monday May 3rd, there was a candlelit procession up South Street from the old chapel to the new church, followed by the blessing of the new building. The Archbishop of Westminster formally opened it on the next day and after the ceremony, there was a luncheon at the Public Hall for 150 people.

---

[40] *Minute Book of the Managers of St Mary's RC Boys School 1903-1943* UNPUBLISHED.

As the building was free of debt, thanks to the generosity of Mrs. Macdonnell, consecration followed quickly in 1910. With the new building, the dedication was again modified, this time to *Our Lady of Sorrows and St. Bridget of Sweden*.

The church is in the Italian Renaissance style. It was built to the design of E. Doran Webb [1864-1915] by Messrs. Erwood and Morris of Bath. It is of brick and stone construction. The stone is oolitic limestone from a quarry near Bath. The bricks are of a bright terra cotta colour but, unfortunately, they are porous which led to the decision in the 1970s to clad the brickwork in roughcast. The roof is flat.

The street facade is decorated with a large low-relief sculpture of the Crucifixion and in the round arch over the front door is a smaller relief depicting the Annunciation.

Inside, the church is basilican in plan with a semicircular apse containing the sanctuary. The ceiling is a barrel vault pierced by dormer windows. The altar and baldachino [the canopy over the altar] are mainly of marble and were made in Italy. The nave is flanked by Corinthian columns, as are the side bays. The carving of the capitals of some of the columns in the side bays remains incomplete. This may be due to the funds running out or alternatively to the impact of the First World War on non-essential work.

Doran Webb had been the architect of the Birmingham Oratory, which was built a few years before the Isleworth church. Although the Oratory is an altogether grander building, the Isleworth church bears a strong family resemblance to it and the design appears be a simplified version of it. The design of the Oratory is reportedly based on the church of San Martino ai Monti in Rome, though the similarities appear limited.

Whatever its inspiration, the building is exotic. It is also impressive. A visiting Quaker was overheard to remark: "They [i.e. the Catholics] do this kind of thing rather well, don't they". The choice of an Italian model rather than, perhaps, Gothic may have been deliberate attempt to emphasise loyalty to Rome but it also has practical value. It offers a unified space with clear sight lines, which encourages greater direct involvement of the congregation in the services. It has also proved more adaptable to changes in the liturgy over the years than a building in the Gothic style might have done.

From the opening of the new church in 1909, the number of Sunday Masses and other services gradually increased. These changes became necessary as the congregation grew along with the local general population and were possible because two and sometimes three assistant priests were based at Isleworth in the period from 1930 until the late 1960s.

## THE FAITH OF OUR FATHERS

Father Green's third major innovation, the annual procession and pilgrimage in honour of the Isleworth martyrs was first held in 1907. It was a joint effort by the Isleworth community and the Guild of Our Lady of Ransom. It continued until the early 1970s. It was a demonstration of the growing confidence of the Catholic community and of its acceptance in the district. It was also a self-conscious imitation of continental Catholic practice - Father Green had lived in Belgium as a student. To understand the background to this manifestation of religious devotion, it is necessary to look back to events in Isleworth in the later Middle Ages.

## Syon Abbey

In 1415, King Henry V launched an ambitious scheme of religious renewal in England. The plan was for a complex of three new monasteries to be located in the vicinity of the royal palace of Sheen. In the event only two were completed – the Charterhouse of Sheen on the Surrey bank of the Thames[41] and Syon Abbey in Isleworth. Syon was to be staffed by the Bridgettine Order, which had originated in Sweden. The spirit of the Order combined the active and the contemplative life and the abbey was intended from the outset to be an instrument of spiritual renewal, a place of pilgrimage, a source of powerful preaching and the publisher of works of spiritual literature.

The community was intended to comprise 60 nuns and 25 men, priests and brothers, living in separate enclosures but sharing a chapel. It was by far the largest and best-endowed nunnery in England and the recently discovered foundations of the chapel revealed a church that may have been almost as large as Westminster Abbey.[42] Henry V had a strong personal devotion to St. Bridget. He funded much of the building work from his private wealth rather than the Exchequer, despite a considerable cost overrun, and laid the foundation stone himself. The national importance of the work is indicated by the fact that Henry's successors throughout the Wars of the Roses, both Yorkist and Lancastrian, continued the work he had begun. The monastery was active from about 1420 and moved to its final site in what is now Syon Park in 1431. Its church was consecrated in 1488.

---

[41] The site is now occupied by the Royal Mid-Surrey Golf Course. A case of one 'religion' replacing another?

[42] Work begun by Channel Four's *Time Team* and continued by Birkbeck College.

The monastery was closed and demolished at the Reformation but many of the nuns stayed together and went into exile. After several moves around Europe, precipitated by political and religious upheavals, the nuns finally returned to England and their community has survived until recently.

The Talbot family had a long and close association with Syon Abbey. The only example of a lay person being admitted as a confrere of the community is John Talbot, the 2nd Earl of Shrewsbury [c.1417-1460].[43] Then in 1836, another John Talbot, the 16th Earl, gave refuge and assistance to Syon nuns on their return to England from the Continent.

Although little of the monastery remains above ground, its site being partly occupied by Syon House, the Isleworth Catholics never forgot it and their chapel and later their church were dedicated to the Swedish Saint who had founded the Bridgettine Order.

Saint Bridget [Birgitta] is an ecumenical saint. She is recognized and revered by the Catholic, Anglican and Lutheran Churches. In 1999, the then Pope declared St. Bridget a patron of Europe.

### The Isleworth Martyrs

The Isleworth Martyrs are Richard Reynolds and John Haile. In 1535, Haile, a secular priest, was the Vicar of Isleworth[44] and Reynolds was one of the monks of Syon Abbey. This was a time of the crisis for the church because the King, Henry VIII, unable to secure from Rome an annulment of his marriage to Catherine of Aragon, had bypassed Papal jurisdiction by making himself supreme head on earth of the English church.

---

[43] Tait M. *A Fair Place – Syon Abbey 1415-1539.* CATTO 2013. A confrere is an associate member of the community who remains in the world but identifies with the work of the Abbey.
[44] Also Rector of Cranford and a canon of Wingham College in Kent.

Most of the leading figures in church and state complied, many of them no doubt taking the view that this was a short-term political expedient, but a few took a principled stand against this assault on the unity of the church. Among them were Sir Thomas More the former Lord Chancellor, John Fisher the Bishop of Rochester, the priors of three Carthusian monasteries, [John Houghton, Augustine Webster and Robert Lawrence], and from Isleworth, Richard Reynolds and John Haile. The three priors, Reynolds and Haile were tried together. The monks were accused of speaking against the supremacy and Haile was accused of stirring up opposition to the King's policies. The government considered both offences high treason and punishable by death. At the trial, the jury initially showed great reluctance to convict but eventually gave way under pressure. The three priors, Reynolds and Haile were all executed at Tyburn on the 4th May 1535. Fisher and More were tried, condemned and executed later in that year.[45] Reynolds and Haile were beatified in 1886. Reynolds was canonized in 1970. More and Fisher had been canonized in 1935.

## The Procession

Hundreds of people joined the procession, which followed a route from St. Bridget's church along South Street, Church Street, Park Road and Twickenham Road to Gumley House, passing places associated with the lives of the martyrs. At Church Street was All Saints' the historic parish church of which John Haile had been vicar. In Park Road were the gates of Syon Park, the site of Syon Abbey where Reynolds spent his religious life and at Busch Corner was the crossroads where

---

[45] Johnston F. R. *Saint Richard Reynolds* SOUTH BRENT 1970; Chambers R. W. *Thomas More* HARMONDSWORTH 1963

two other martyrs had been put to death in 1588.[46] The procession was a grand affair with representatives of all the local Catholic parishes, bands, local church organizations and guilds, Scouts and Guides. There were teams of men carrying statues of the martyrs shoulder high on wooden cradles and schoolchildren in white each carrying a bead of a giant rosary made of wood and painted gold.

The police halted the traffic and the local population turned out to watch the spectacle as it passed. The procession was cited in the canonization process for Richard Reynolds as evidence of strong local devotion to the martyrs.

*Part of the annual procession in honour of the Isleworth Martyrs – about 1955*

At the time of its inauguration, Catholic processions could be intensely controversial. A procession of the Blessed Eucharist in the streets around Westminster Cathedral had been planned in connection with the 1908 Eucharistic Congress.[47] Father Green was chairman of the processions committee for the Congress and he may have regarded the Isleworth procession as a prototype or dress rehearsal for the Westminster event. The prospect of a procession in Westminster provoked a nervous

---

[46] James Claxton a secular priest and Thomas Felton a student for the priesthood.
[47] Eucharistic Congresses are religious gatherings intended to encourage popular devotion to the Holy Eucharist and frequent Communion. They comprise ceremonies, lectures, discussions and processions.

reaction from the government who asked that it should be a low-key affair with "all elements of ecclesiastical ceremonial" removed. The church complied.

One of the Vatican officials attending the 1908 Congress was a certain Mgr. Eugenio Pacelli who came as assistant to the Cardinal Secretary of State.[48] He was in England again in 1911, this time as a member of the Papal delegation to the coronation of King George V.[49] It was during this visit that the future pope came to visit Isleworth to renew an acquaintance with Father Green formed at the Eucharistic Congress.


## THE FIRST WORLD WAR

The First World War hit the community hard. In all nearly four hundred Isleworth men were killed and among them were fifty-three Catholics, most of them of Irish origin.

Notable among the Isleworth men who died in the war was Serjeant Harry Shea, of the Grenadier Guards, the only son of Philip and Mary Shea, who lived in Worton Road. He was a professional soldier and was killed in the fighting around Ypres in Flanders in October 1914, leaving a young widow, Hilda. It was not all loss; one of the former pupils of St. Mary's School, Andrew Edwards, won the Military Medal.[50]

Father Green was summoned at short notice in March 1915 to act as a full time Officiating Roman Catholic Chaplain in the Royal Naval Division, leaving his assistant Father O'Brien in charge at Isleworth.[51] Concern had been growing about the

[48] Mgr Pacelli was elected pope in 1939, taking the name Pius XII.
[49] Hatch A. and Walshe S. *Crown of Glory – The Life of Pope Pius XII.* LONDON 1957.
[50] *Minute Book of the Managers of St. Mary's RC Boys School 1903-1943* UNPUBLISHED.
[51] Taylor G. *The Sea Chaplains* OXFORD 1978.

shortage of Catholic chaplains in the Royal Navy. In February 1915 a high level meeting between the Admiralty, the Church and some interested Members of Parliament, led to the rushed appointment of additional priests, among them Father Green, to serve with the Navy.

The Royal Naval Division was made up of sailors being deployed as infantry. Father Green served with them at Gallipoli and in France, bringing the sacraments to sailors in the front line in appalling and dangerous conditions. Contemporary accounts lay stress on the ecumenical spirit engendered by the shared adversity of war. One priest is described as walking among the wounded, arm in arm with the Presbyterian chaplain. Father Green himself was invalided back to England twice, first from Gallipoli with dysentery and later from France with an injury to his heel. He returned, exhausted, to Isleworth in September 1915.[52]

Percy House, part of the Brentford Union Workhouse complex in the Twickenham Road, was used as a military hospital during the war.[53] Nearly 5,000 wounded soldiers were treated there and two votive plaques in the church bear testimony to recoveries made in 1916 and 1917.

Father Green's wartime experiences led to him being instrumental in the formation after the war of the Isleworth branch of the British Legion. A committee on which two parishioners, Mr. Murphy and Mr. Weathers, served organized the erection in 1922 of the town war memorial, which is sited in the square outside the church and was designed in a style sympathetic to the façade of the church. The members of

---

[52] For a fuller account of Father Green's experiences see *The Honeslaw Chronicle* Journal of the Hounslow and District History Society Spring Edition 2011.
[53] London Borough of Hounslow *Isleworth As It Was* NELSON 1982.

the Catholic community who died are also identified on the memorial plaque inside the church, which was unveiled by Viscount Fitzalan in 1925.

With the publication of the new Code of Canon Law in 1918, existing missions like Isleworth became regularly constituted parishes.

Father Green died unexpectedly in 1929 but not before a tower had been added to the church, as well as a hall known as the Guild Hall. Previously the parish had been a frequent user of the Isleworth Public Hall for functions and meetings.[54]

It is a measure of Father Green's standing in the district that local clergy from the Church of England and the Free Churches as well as civic leaders attended his funeral.

*The della Robbia style roundel set in the front wall of the parish hall*

## THE TOWER AND THE BELL

When the new church was built provision was made for a bell tower. The foundations and ground floor structure were provided in the original construction adjacent to and north of the façade. In the event, the tower was not built until 1927.

[54] Heston & Isleworth Council Baths and Fire Brigade Committee minutes.

The bell is dedicated to the Archangel Michael. It is a memorial to two late Victorian writers, Katherine Bradley and Edith Cooper, aunt and niece, who were prolific authors of poetry and verse drama under the joint pen name of *Michael Field*. They were inseparable companions who lived, wrote, and travelled together from 1887 until their deaths in 1913-14. Their spiritual journey took them from the Church of England, through paganism and aestheticism to Catholicism. Unlike other former aesthetes who became Catholics, for them conversion seems to have been a fulfilment rather than a rejection of their past lives. Although they lived in Richmond, they often attended St. Bridget's church and were friends with Father Green. Miss Bradley was a regular visitor to patients in the consumption [i.e. tuberculosis] wards at West Middlesex Hospital. Her confessor, the famous Dominican friar, Father Vincent McNabb, came to preach at the opening ceremony of the new church in 1909. The companions died within a few months of each other, the younger woman in December 1913 and the older in September 1914. They share a grave in the Catholic graveyard at Mortlake. Miss Bradley left £400 "for the poor of Isleworth" to be distributed by Father Green.

The construction of the bell tower at St. Bridget's provided the opportunity for their friends to create a memorial appropriate to the poets in that it had a 'voice' which could be heard throughout the neighbourhood. The bell was cast by the Whitechapel Bell Foundry in 1926. The Auxiliary Bishop of Westminster dedicated it to St. Michael the Archangel in an elaborate and dramatic traditional ceremony on January 11th 1927 in the nave of the church. It was subsequently installed in the tower. It has recently been restored and Michael's voice can again be heard in Isleworth.

The bell is inaccessible but its dedication deserves to be better known, so I reproduce the inscription here:

IN MEMORIAM MICHAELIS FIELD POETAE

{RUTH BRADLEY EDITH COOPER}

IN AETERNUM CORAM DEO MICHAEL CANTA

FLOS UT IN ARVO SIC HOMO PARVO TEMPORE FLEVIT

MOX DATA CAELIS VOX MICHAELIS MORTE CIEBIT

This may be freely translated as:

*In memory of Michael Field, the poets*

*{Ruth Bradley Edith Cooper}.*

*Sing, Michael, in the presence of God forever.*

*We perish like the flower in the field, so for a while there is weeping; but before long the voice of Michael from Heaven shall waken the dead.*

Shortly after Father Green's arrival, another prolific Catholic author had made his home in Isleworth. Andrew Hilliard Atteridge was a war correspondent, military historian and biographer. One of his books, a collected biography of Napoleon's brothers, originally issued in 1909, the year he came to Isleworth, has not been surpassed and was recently reprinted. He was an active member of the congregation and early historian of the parish but his manuscript was never published.

# CONSOLIDATION

Father Green was succeeded by Father Francis Rusher who like Father Green had previously served at Westminster. He continued his predecessor's work until his death in 1950.

In the Thirties, new parishes were founded from Isleworth at East Twickenham [St. Margaret's] in 1930 and at Osterley [St. Vincent's] in 1936. The Osterley church building [now used as the parish hall] had been built as a chapel-of-ease to Isleworth in 1933.[55] The first marriage held at St. Margaret's church [in April 1931] was, appropriately enough, between an Isleworth bridegroom and a St. Margaret's bride.

As part of a programme of new building undertaken by the Diocese of Westminster in the 1930s a large new rectory was built beside the church. Anthony Wareing and Mgr Weld had lived at Shrewsbury Place. When the site on the Twickenham Road was acquired, the clergy lived in an old house there. This was demolished when the new rectory was built.

# WORLD WAR TWO AND AFTER

The Second World War brought its share of misery and bravery with evacuations, conscription, aerial bombing and rationing.

After the War, the pattern of parish life returned to the cycle of the Church's year. After the great feast of Christmas, Candlemas was celebrated in early February with candle-lit shrines set up in the classrooms of St. Mary's Primary School. It was followed by Ash Wednesday, Lent and Easter. The ancient observation of the Easter Triduum was revived throughout the Roman Church in 1955 and St. Bridget's duly adopted the ceremonies.

---

[55] Weiler T. *A Parish History 1936-1996 St Vincent de Paul, Osterley* OSTERLEY 1996.

The 1st May was the occasion for the Crowning of Mary, Queen of the May. The privilege of placing the crown on the head of the statue of Our Lady, which was set up in the nave of the church and surrounded by flowers and candles, was given each year to one of the girls from the school.

*The clergy in the early 1950s: the Rector Father Gomes (3rd from left) with his assistant priests (left to right) Father Haines, Father Dempsey and Father O'Leary*

On the Feast of Corpus Christi, which usually fell in June, there was an outdoor procession within the grounds of the church or Gumley House with pride of place being given to children who had received their First Communion that year. In July each year there was the Martyr's Procession which continued until the mid-1970s by which time it was reduced to a walk along the pavements because traffic levels were such that road closures were no longer practical. In 1970 the canonization of Richard Reynolds was finally achieved. The parishioners celebrated the canonization with a pageant based on events surrounding the martyrdom.

Father Manoel Gomes, a native of British Guiana [now Guyana], served as parish priest from 1950 to 1957. He was succeeded by Father Charles Connor, a Londoner. Their curates did pastoral work in the parish and acted as chaplains to the convents, the lay associations and the West Middlesex Hospital.

At this time preparation for the sacraments of confession, communion and confirmation was undertaken within the school by the teachers and there was close integration of school and parish life.

Among the lay associations were the Legion of Mary, the Society of St. Vincent de Paul and the Union of Catholic Mothers, as well as Guide and Scout troops and a youth club. The choir that provided the music for the Sung Mass each Sunday was led by the organist Miss Theresa Costloe. The members of the choir were involved in other parish activities notably the annual garden fête.

*Alderman 'Snowy' Fielder opens the annual garden fete in 1958, the year in which he was Mayor of the Borough.*

*The choir in fancy dress for a garden fete. Miss Costloe on the right.*

The involvement of Catholics in local affairs never matched that of the early part of the century but veteran Council member Alderman A. J. Fielder, who had served on the Borough Council since its inception in 1932, continued to be a voice in local affairs. Alderman Fielder, known to all as 'Snowy', was a Justice of the Peace and was elected Mayor in 1958.

The Second Vatican Ecumenical Council [1963-1965] had little immediate impact on Isleworth but the liturgical reforms that followed led to significant changes in the externals of worship and a substantial reordering of the layout of the church interior. Solemn High Masses with plainchant and motets sung by the choir were replaced by a Family Mass with simpler congregational singing. While the translation of the liturgy into English was accepted fairly readily, as had been the introduction of the dialogue Mass[56] in the late 1950s, influential members of the congregation resisted the changes to the church interior required by the reformed liturgy. Consequently the reordering of the church interior begun by Father Connor proceeded only slowly over a number of years.

Another consequence of the changing practice of the church in general was the transfer of preparation for the sacraments from the school to the parish, with greater direct parental involvement.

The defensiveness which had characterised the English Catholic church's attitude towards other Christian communities was slow to dissolve and could still be encountered locally as late as the early 1960s in, for example, a reluctance to engage in ecumenical contacts.[57] However, as part of the aggiornamento

---

[56] In the dialogue Mass, the entire congregation was encouraged to make the Latin responses previously made only by the altar server.
[57] Author's recollection.

or updating initiated by Pope John XXIII, the Catholic Church in England agreed in 1966 to take part in a national ecumenical initiative launched by the British Council of Churches called *The People Next Door*. This was a programme of six meetings at weekly intervals in which lay people from the various local churches met in each other's homes for prayer and discussion of their faith and experience. In Isleworth it forged contacts and friendships that have lasted over the years. It played a significant part in the thawing of relations between the various Christian communities. Previously the only inter-church activity in which the Catholics had been involved was the annual Remembrance Service at the War Memorial.

Another powerful laity-led ecumenical initiative of the late 1960s with considerable St. Bridget's involvement was the Hounslow World Poverty Action Group whose campaign for more aid and fairer trade engaged all the local Christian communities. It culminated, as the 1970 general election approached, in what was described as the largest political meeting to have been held in the Borough for many years. In the new Gumley House school hall, in front of an audience of about 500 local Christians, the sitting MP and the rival parliamentary candidates were pressed to commit themselves to taking action on world development.

That there had been movement in relations with other churches is demonstrated by the modification to the annual procession that took place in the early 1970s. For years the All Saints' Church of England parish had been inviting the Catholics to take part in joint activities. In 1973, the Vicar at All Saints invited the Catholics to say Mass in his church on the day that the martyrs were remembered. This time the invitation was accepted and a new era of friendship emerged.

At about this time St. Bridget's also began a friendship with the Isleworth Congregational Church that has endured and found expression in the prayer group on which both communities are strongly represented.

St. Bridget's can legitimately claim to be the mother church for West Middlesex and for the period 1994 to 2001, it acted again as a mother church when the Area Bishop decided to base himself in Isleworth. The then Archbishop, Cardinal Hume, had decided that his Assistant Bishops should be allocated to specific areas of the diocese. These Area Bishops were to live in the locality for which they were responsible. Isleworth came under the West Area. The first Area Bishop [Gerald Mahon] had lived in a house in Chiswick but had based his support team in surplus accommodation on the Gumley House site. When Bishop Mahon died, his successor, Bishop Patrick O'Donoghue decided to live at the rectory at Isleworth. He was officially the Parish Priest but his episcopal duties meant that he had to rely on assistant priests to serve the parish. This arrangement came to an end when Bishop Patrick was appointed to the Diocese of Lancaster in 2001 and pastoral care by a parish priest was resumed.

In 2000 the parish celebrated the advent of the new Millennium with a special Mass and the redecoration of the interior of the church. The refurbishment was continued and completed for the centenary of the present church building in 2009.

In 2008 the St. Bridget's Parish Pastoral Council decided to mark the 100th anniversary of the completion of the present church building. It was not only an occasion for celebration but also an opportunity to renew parish life and cement relationships with the local sister churches and the wider community in the town.

An ambitious year-long programme of events and activities was devised embracing religious services, pilgrimages, social functions, concerts, publications, lectures and improvements to the parish plant.

By coincidence 2009 was an anniversary for two of the sister churches. The members of the Isleworth Congregational Church were celebrating the 160th anniversary of the foundation of their church in 1849 and the All Saints' Isleworth Anglican parish was celebrating the 40th anniversary of the rebuilding of their church after a disastrous fire. The churches collaborated and the celebrations became ecumenical.

Recognising the importance of modern communications, the opportunity was taken to rebuild and relaunch the parish website and transform the weekly newsletter. Both website and newsletter subsequently won awards in a competition organized by Westminster Archdiocese.

The centenary activities received warm coverage in the local and church press. They were a worthy celebration of the vigorous life of the parish and succeeded in strengthening links with the sister churches and the wider Isleworth community.

## REFLECTION

The Isleworth Catholic community is not a typical Catholic community. For one thing, it is very old. The great majority of present-day Catholic parishes in England were founded in the course of the last 150 years. Isleworth looks back on 300 years of continuous existence. For another it is not in an area of traditional Catholic strength like some parts of Lancashire and the North East. In fact West Middlesex was in many ways unpromising territory for the revival of Catholic Christianity which had been effectively extinguished in this area for 150 years following the Reformation, although there were of course individual Catholics living in the vicinity from time to time.

Furthermore, it was not founded, as most were, by a zealous priest or lay patron but grew organically out of a domestic chaplaincy. In other places, the departure of the Catholic family that had supported the chaplain resulted in the ending of the provision of Catholic services. In Isleworth the mission survived the departure of the Talbots and grew. Unlike other Catholic communities, it has never has been dominated by one social class or immigrant group and this I believe has been a source of strength.

The town of Isleworth developed during the Nineteenth and Twentieth Centuries both as a dormitory suburb of London and an industrial and commercial area in its own right. There was, through an accident of history, a well-established mission with its own schools ready and able to serve the Catholics among the expanding population. It was, I believe, a case of the tiny Isleworth mission being in the right place at the right time from the 1820s onwards to serve, and grow with, an expanding population of which a significant minority was either already Catholic or had joined the Church.

## POSTSCRIPT

The past importance of the Isleworth mission is demonstrated by the fact that clergy of the calibre of Richard Kendal, Anthony Wareing, Francis Weld and Eric Green were content to serve here for most of their priestly lives. Weld in particular belonged to a wealthy and influential family and had the opportunity to spend his life in the Curia in Rome but chose to return to his native land and serve the Isleworth mission for 44 years.

Isleworth has never been a wealthy parish but it has benefited materially over the years from the generosity of many people including the Talbot family, Mgr. Weld, the Misses Saunders and Mrs. Macdonnell. More importantly, it has benefited spiritually from the ministry and prayers of the clergy and nuns who have served here and the devotion of generations of lay people. Nor should we forget those staunch individuals, most of them women, who have been custodians of the memory of the parish and a source of continuity when change has occurred.

I am aware that any telling of the story of our community could never cover in detail all the people who have contributed and all the events that have shaped the parish. Nevertheless, I hope this booklet will remind longstanding members of the community of our history and give newcomers, visitors and anyone interested some sense of how we came to be here.

The purpose of the Church is to bring people to understand and respond to God's unconditional love and reflect that love within the parish and the wider community.  In the present situation where the parish depends for the sacraments and pastoral care on a single priest, supported by a retired colleague, the burden of maintaining the Catholic community in Isleworth falls increasingly on the shoulders of the lay people. This booklet shows that we are heirs to a great tradition and it will, I hope, encourage us to live up to our Christian vocation.

# ACKNOWLEDGEMENTS

*I gratefully acknowledge help received from:*

*Father Gerard King*

*Father Stewart Hasker*

*Mary and Kevin Brown*

*The Sisters, Faithful Companions of Jesus at Gumley House*

*The Poor Sisters of Nazareth formerly at Nazareth House*

*The Little Company of Mary*

*The Carmelite Community of the Holy Family*

*The Catholic Record Society*

*The Catholic National Library*

*The National Archives (formerly the Public Record Office)*

*Gilda Bagnall who drew the sketches*

# Author's Note on Sources

This study originated in the collection of material for an exhibition held at St. Bridget's as part of the Millennium Celebrations in 2000. Since then I have made further investigations which have enabled me to expand and in some cases correct the story that the exhibition told. I have had to rely heavily on secondary sources because the original parish and mission records are so meagre. St. Bridget's is not and as far as I can tell never has been particularly interested in paperwork and perhaps that is as it should be. Furthermore, what records there were have not generally been preserved in the parish or anywhere accessible. Nevertheless I believe the story compiled from the available material is both convincing and worth telling. I have used such primary records as have survived, supplemented by published sources as indicated in the footnotes. The principal published source for the early history of the mission is the article in the Catholic Record Society CRS Miscellanea XIII. This was in turn used as the basis for the article in the Victoria County History of Middlesex (Volume III).

To my knowledge, two earlier attempts at producing a history of the parish have been made, neither of which were published; the first in the early 1900s by Andrew Atteridge, the second in the 1960s by J. G. Castle who used the Atteridge manuscript as his principal source. (Atteridge A. H. *The Catholic Church in Isleworth 1085-1909* and Castle J. G. *Some Notes on the Catholics of Isleworth 1966*). My approach has been somewhat different from theirs in that I have concerned myself exclusively with the history of the Post-Reformation Catholic community centred on Isleworth. Although Atteridge's work was not published in its entirety, it did form the basis for a pamphlet published each year as a service sheet for the annual outdoor procession.

# Appendix 1: THE CLERGY[58]

| Dates | Name | Notes |
|---|---|---|
| To 1744 | John Matthews | Chaplain and Missioner |
| 1744-1759 | Richard Kendal | Chaplain and Missioner |
| 1759-1778 | John Exley | Chaplain and Missioner |
| 1778-1790 | Robert Tommins | Chaplain and Missioner |
| 1790-1810 | William Allan S. J. | Chaplain and Missioner |
| 1810-1854 | Anthony Wareing | Missioner |
| 1854-1898 | Francis Weld | Missionary Rector |
| 1898-1906 | Thomas Gorman | Missionary Rector |
| 1906-1929 | Eric Green | To 1918, Missionary Rector From 1918, Parish Priest |
| 1929-1950 | Francis Rusher | Parish Priest |
| 1951-1957 | Manoel Gomes | Parish Priest |
| 1958-1969 | Charles Connor | Parish Priest |
| 1970-1975 | Albert Davey | Parish Priest |
| 1976-1988 | Cedric Stanley | Parish Priest |
| 1989-1991 | Charles Mercer | Parish Priest |
| 1992-1994 | John Seabrook | Parish Priest |
| 1994-2001 | Patrick O'Donoghue | Bishop in West Area and Parish Priest. Pastoral care of the parish during this period was provided by: 1994-1996: Duncan Adamson 1996-2001: Gerard King |
| 2001-2003 | Neil Burrows | Parish Priest |
| 2003-date | Stewart Hasker | Priest in Charge |

[58] To 1906 CRS Miscellanea XIII, from 1906 Catholic Directory annual.

# Appendix 2: TIMELINE

1675     Suggested date of origin of the mission. Shrewsbury House or Place first occupied by a member of the Catholic Talbot family. Lost registers supposed to date from this year.

1743     Bishop Challoner visits Shrewsbury Place to confirm 23 people.

1746     First entry in surviving register.

1758     The Vestry (the local authority) issues a writ alleging that a Catholic chapel has been in use at Shrewsbury Place for 30 years and requiring the chapel closed and the priest to leave. The Brentford magistrates throw out the case.

1767     The Bishop of London's Return of Papists lists 1 priest, 28 male and 31 female Catholics as resident in the Parish of Isleworth. This is the 3rd largest concentration in Middlesex.

1770     Shrewsbury Place in use as a boys school with 60 pupils, all Catholics.

1778     First Catholic Relief Act - decriminalises the Catholic priesthood.

1779     Second Relief Act - permits churches, chapels and schools.

1797     Shrewsbury Place demolished. A free-standing chapel provided for the mission by Lord Shrewsbury.

1810     Anthony Wareing is appointed priest for the mission and the Sunday congregation numbers about 20.

1829     Catholic emancipation – restoration of most civil rights to Catholics.

1841     Madame d'Houet acquires Gumley House as a convent for her Faithful Companions of Jesus and opens two girls' schools - a private boarding school and a poor school for the children of the town; the forerunners of Gumley and St. Mary's schools respectively.

1850     Restoration of the Catholic hierarchy in England and Wales.

| | |
|---|---|
| 1851 | National census of religious practice finds Anthony Wareing still the priest and 70-80 people worshipping regularly at St. Bridget's. |
| 1854 | New Rector Mgr. Francis Weld opens a poor school for boys adjacent to the chapel. |
| 1855 | Mgr. Weld provides a new chapel at his own expense. |
| 1892 | Isleworth House is bought as a convent for the Poor Sisters of Nazareth and renamed Nazareth House. |
| 1906 | Father Eric Green becomes Rector. |
| 1907 | Father Green begins the annual Martyrs or Outdoor Procession. |
| 1908 | New Boys' School opened at Twickenham Road/South Street on land given by the Misses Saunders of Silver Hall. |
| 1909 | New church built next to the Boys' School. Paid for by Mrs. Macdonnell of Nazareth House. |
| 1910 | New church consecrated. Children's home and chapel built at Nazareth House. |
| 1922 | Clock Tower War Memorial opened. |
| 1925 | War memorial inside the church unveiled by the Viscount Fitzalan. |
| 1926 | Tower added to new church. |
| 1927 | Bell installed and dedicated to St. Michael in memory of the poets 'Michael Field'. |
| Late 1920s | Guild Hall added. |
| 1935 | New rectory built. |
| 1970 | Canonization of Isleworth Martyr, Richard Reynolds. |
| 2002 | Nazareth House closes. |
| 2009 | Centenary of the opening of the present church celebrated. |
| 2015 | 600th anniversary of the foundation of Syon Abbey. |

# Index

# Notes

# Notes